JAY MAISEL

Gruppo Editoriale Fabbri

by Emily L. Vickers

A SPECTRUM BOOK

THE GREAT PHOTOGRAPHERS
JAY MAISEL

Prentice-Hall, Inc., Englewood Cliffs, New Jersey 07632

JAY MAISEL

By Emily L. Vickers

Self-portrait of Jay Maisel

Art critics have long acknowledged the expressive limitations of the individual, straight, unmanipulated photograph. A painter can make a statement in a single painting. The straight photographer speaks through a number of images. For this reason, many photographers' works are best considered in groups.

The book you hold in your hands is a collection of photographs by Jay Maisel. It barely scratches the surface of the photographer's life's work and the statement it makes is one of a visual eclecticism that defies specification. The binding principle here is not narrative, subject matter, social outlook, or moral statement. It is one man's view of the beauty he finds in a thousand places—some places whose association with beauty is incongruous, all places where the beauty was there to begin with, and is still there if one cares to look. Jay Maisel cares to look. In a sense he can't help looking. He admits he is "helpless in the face of beauty," and yet he has difficulty describing beauty in the abstract. He knows, though, where to find it.

"There are so many things that excite me visually, the infinite variety of the human face, the interrelationships of people, nature in all seasons, the structures and environments man builds, and overall, the light, the shifting light and the nuances it brings to color."

For thirty years, Maisel has been collecting beauty in these and all other forms that excite him visually. The photographs in this volume are a few, chosen thoughtfully by the editors. Inasmuch as subtlety of colors is lost in reproduction, the presentation of images maintaining fidelity to the original is difficult to achieve even in the most carefully produced photography books.

To realize the magnitude of Jay Maisel's body of work, as well as his enormous success in photography, it is necessary to visit his studio— "the Bank." In fact, the more you learn about Jay Maisel and the building on New York's Bowery he has owned and occupied for the past eighteen years, the harder it is to imagine one without the other; their symbiosis is complete. Most people, particularly space-conscious New Yorkers, are flabbergasted by the idea of one person owning and occupying (in the sense of a liquid filling its container) every square foot of a six-story former bank. When you spend time there with the owner the space seems smaller, the idea of total occupancy less outrageous. It is the domain of an eccentric pack-rat collector who readily admits to having the soul of a janitor.

After negotiating the front steps (gingerly avoiding any of the neighborhood bums who may be napping there) an invited guest will be greeted at the huge oak double doors by one of six Maisel staff members. On those occasions when Maisel is in town and not out shooting pictures, he might answer the door himself, cigar tipped up F.D.R.-style, dressed just slightly up-scale from his prostrate neighbors outside. Once inside, the contrast is staggering—like Ali Baba stumbling into the cave of the forty thieves. As your eyes adjust to the dimness, floodlights begin to pop like flashbulbs in sequence around the room, illuminating a gigantic space 34 feet wide and 72 feet long, with an articulated ceiling 20 feet from the floor, the former main banking floor of the Germania Bank. Except for two large steel-doored vaults at the end of the room, few remaining details give away its former function, although the mosaic tiled floor, gilded moldings on marble walls, and leaded-glass windows clearly belong to an earlier age of grandeur. Descriptions of the main room at Jay Maisel's studio invariably include the paradoxical presence of a basketball backboard and halfcourt at the entrance to the room. Jay still shoots a few baskets now and then, when he's under pressure from jobs or trying to give up tobacco, but the basketball hoop serves another purpose as well. It separates those who came to see Jay Maisel, the photographer, from those who came for the "phenomenon" of Maisel the high-priced grand wizard of commercial photography. Anyone who ignores the net in favor of dozens of exquisite dye transfer prints lining the walls wins points immediately with the photographer. At first it looks like a group show, the variety of themes and subjects could be the work of a number of photographers, not just one, and it takes many hours of looking to delineate the delicate web of continuity binding the whole. Asked to describe the "Maisel style," the photographer dodges the question by saying "That's like asking me how I smell—it's not for me to say. You must make that kind of judgment yourself."

So you begin to look. A sweeping aerial photograph of New York funnels the eye into a deep space between a sheet of low-hanging clouds and the spikes of architecture below. Two trees with branches as delicate as bridal lace covered with frost shiver under an ice-blue Italian sky. A flock of pigeons fly in concentric formation, their earth-toned feathers blending with the muddy brown city sky. More birds, a frequent counterpoint in Maisel's compositions, perch within the inner window frame of a Portuguese peasant house; the bright yellow outer frame vibrates against the rough brushstrokes of the blue façade. This is Maisel's often-published "Blue Wall with Doves," and printed 40 inches by 60 inches. The image effectively anchors one wall of this huge room. There are many façades among these pictures, many images where space is denied, foregrounds and backgrounds merging. This viewpoint is rectilinear, strictly frontal in orientation, even confrontational. The author of these pictures has made no attempt to approach the subject from an angle, and yet the straightforward approach is not intimidating, not aggressive. The subjects seem to respond pliantly, trustingly, like the little boy behind the window screen in Baja California, framed by chintz curtains and a light as soft as the expression in his eyes. You could spend hours at one wall, but the tour moves on. The second floor of the Bank has lower ceilings than the main room;

the all-white walls and gray linoleum floors create a more conventional gallery space. Nothing distracts the eye from dozens of 40-inch x 60-inch prints that line these walls. No image from downstairs is repeated and each print is box-mounted and arranged to maximum effect among its neighbors. By the time you reach the third floor, where a long corridor opens into nine small rooms filled with hundreds more prints, the Bank's unified form and function become apparent. The perfect blend of pragmatism and egotistic self-indulgence, Maisel has created a permanent showcase of his work for clients and print collectors, as well as the largest private gallery in New York devoted to the work of one artist. By now, even the visitor who came with preconceptions or fair warnings is either overwhelmed by the enormity of the ego that produced this spectacle or genuinely impressed. Few are bored and even fewer are not curious about when, how, and why it all came about.

In a sense, Maisel and the Bank beg the old chicken-and-egg question. Did Jay's ambition and success allow him to create this magnificent environment or did his high overhead, along with so much available space, necessitate and encourage his appetite for financial success and collections of all kinds—especially his own photographs? The truth is probably a little of both. When Jay bought the building in 1966 his success as a photographer and his acquisitive nature were already well-established. However, the Bank enabled him to create a comfortable and secure headquarters, a self-contained world filled with his photographs and his "esoteric aesthetica." It also obliged him to work for other people—at high rates—in order to maintain that world. Never one to live hand to mouth, Maisel now literally could not afford to.

Jay Maisel came to photography from a fine-arts background. An early interest in painting and graphics led him to Yale University where he studied color with the Bauhaus master, Josef Albers, and earned a B.F.A., in 1953. He maintains a firm belief in photographic self-education. Although he benefited from his two photography courses with Herbert Matter in 1954 and Alexi Brodovitch in 1956, he warns the beginner against reliance on photography schools, which focus on technique and the past masters of photography to the exclusion of anything else. "There are a lot of one-dimensional photographers out there who believe that the history of photography began with Daguerre, when it really follows a tradition of two-dimensional seeing, which began the first time someone saw a reflection in still water." With this statement, Maisel asserts his position on the photography-as-art question by refusing to see photography as anything but a new medium introduced into the tradition of seeing and expression to which all the visual arts belong. He encourages the study of all art forms, including music and literature, to sharpen sensitivity to life and prevent a stultifying photographic myopia. Likewise, he admonishes young photographers not to follow too closely the styles of other, more successful, shooters. "The big fault is taking photographs of photographs. You've got to develop the aesthetic sense to take your own pictures."

Maisel's own transition from painter to black-and-white photographer to color photographer was a natural progression for one whose energy level and need for instant gratification are legend. Before going to Yale, he studied at Cooper Union in his native New York City. The courses were design-oriented, with an emphasis on highly structured architectural drawing and calligraphy. Despite this architectonic tendency and due to the unavoidable influence of the New York School of Action Painting, Maisel's paintings were sensual abstractions in oils, described once by Morris Kantor as "emotional outbursts." Given Albers' belief in structured control of the medium (he said an artist should be able to paint in a white Palm Beach suit), it is not surprising that the Yale experience did little to encourage Maisel's career as a painter. At the top of the class in color perception, the young student was unable to apply that knowledge to his paintings, according to Albers. In addition, Maisel's own restless personality was incompatible with the nature of painting. Individual paintings required long hours of intense concentration, often without the desired results. Painting simply couldn't provide the constant stream of visual, sensual, and artistic gratification that he required. Enter the camera.

A cooperative project among Yale artists, architects, and philosopher/engineer Buckminster Fuller gave Jay the chance to use a camera (an Exacta borrowed from Fuller) seriously for the first time. He documented the construction of Fuller's dome and discovered the creative possibilities of photography in the process. Although he continued to paint and draw, he finally conceded his temperament was better suited to photography than painting.

"After a while I realized I was sneaking out to take pictures when I should have been painting and drawing. That was in the early '50's. All my contemporaries were painting and drawing, so I had to decide whether I was painting because of peer pressure or because I really wanted to". He now admits that it took him years to get comfortable with the label "photographer." His decision was also based on his desire to support himself through his work, and the market for photography at the time provided him with ample opportunity to do so. After a brief spate of non-photography night jobs, freeing days for taking pictures, Maisel was ready for New York and the commercial art market. His first assignments didn't interfere with his prolific personal shooting, and by 1955 he had mounted his first one-man show. Gradually, however, even black-and-white photography constrained Maisel's creative impulse. His desire to be out shooting pictures surpassed his discipline in the darkroom, and the unprinted film began to mount up. He still has over 5,000 rolls of mostly unprinted black-and-white negatives squirreled away in some dark corner of his building. Once again, the medium failed to keep pace with the artist's need to produce and see results immediately.

Enter the Kodachrome slide. Finally, Maisel could get the visual feedback he wanted. Within twenty-four hours, his original vision could be projected on the wall of his editing room. The distance between concept and completion was now acceptable. Like his previous transition, the switch from black and white to color answered an ideological question for Maisel as well. Although he enjoyed his black-and-white work, it was still too much of an abstraction of the reality he saw and wanted to put on film. A picture that Maisel says oiled his transition to color photography is one of several black-and-white images in his portfolio slide show. The shot is of an American flag suspended beneath a tree in full foliage outside a white clapboard house. Dappled sunlight mingles with shadows on the flag's surface. "We all know that's red, that's white, and that's blue," Maisel points out. "Then why aren't we looking at it like that? Why are we looking at it in reverse of what's really there?" As he says this, the colors seem to assert themselves through the grays of the flag, making Maisel's point visually. "The only thing in the world that looks like a black-and-white photograph is another black-and-white photograph."

An early decision to devote himself to photographing "what's really there" by abandoning black and white in favor of color developed into a complete philosophy based on a confrontation with reality that expresses itself in all of Maisel's work. Like all expressed realities, however, it is one of the artist's choosing. A selection of images from the world as it appears to him. It's a very different world from that of Gary Winogrand or Diane Arbus. Maisel explains: "There is chaos everywhere, but I have no responsibility to reflect this. I have the privilege, the obligation to pick what I like and work with that. I can show garbage or I cannot show garbage. I can show beauty or I can show tragedy: It's my choice."

Choice and selection, rather than imposition and manipulation are the hallmarks of Maisel's philosophy. He doesn't believe in manipulating the image before or after he releases the shutter. He never uses filters in his personal work and he uses them on corporate assignments only to correct for incompatible light sources such as fluorescents. When asked by Pete Turner, famous for his imaginative use of filters, how he achieves such fantastic lighting effects without polarizers or filtration, Maisel responded "I wait."

Waiting for the right time to shoot rather than creating effects artificially is a choice Maisel has made in search of the freshness and spontaneity he considers essential to all aspects of his life. "If I prepare too much, on any level of life—talking, photographing, loving, learning—then what the situation can really give me is lost to my preconceived atti-

(continued on page 57)

THE PHOTOGRAPHS

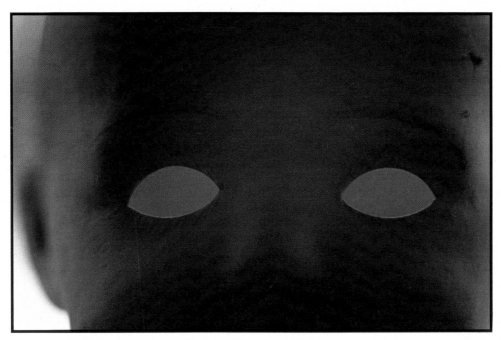

Jackson, Wyoming, 1973

Philippines, 1975

Bermuda, 1967

San Francisco, 1976

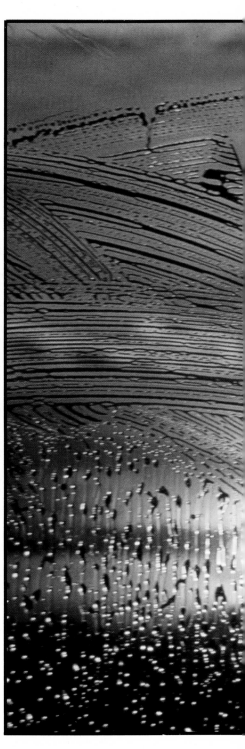

Bogota Airport, Colombia, 1973

From the "New York in Gold" series, New York, 1971

New York, 1971

World Trade Center, New York, 1981

Baja California, Mexico, 1972

Ice Crystals on my Windowpane, 1980

Midwest, U.S.A., 1975

Taken from the helicopter over Rhode Island, U.S.A., 1976

Maine, 1964

Cartagena, Colombia, 1973

Kentucky, 1972

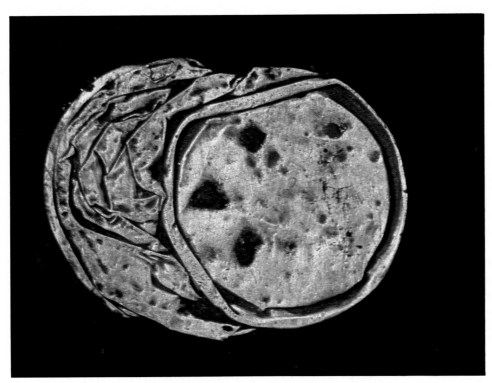

From the "Look Down!" series, New York, 1979

New Mexico, 1968

Coney Island, New York, 1974

Coney Island, New York, 1974

Bahia, Brazil, 1976

Tokyo, 1970

View from helicopter over Seattle, Washington, 1977

Snapshot from a moving car on Franklin D. Roosevelt Drive, New York, 1980

Geneva Switzerland, 1970

Fireworks in Little Italy and Chinatown seen from my window, New York, 1977

Louisiana, 1973

California, 1973

New York, 1972

Bucharest, Romania, 1974

Cheryl Tiegs, Palmas del Mar, Puerto Rico, 1973

Osaka, Japan, 1970

White Woman Suckling Black Baby, San Francisco, 1978

Isfahan, Iran, 1971

Tokyo, 1970

Jerusalem, 1974

Mosque, Isfahan, Iran, 1976

In the High Atlas, Morocco, 1970

Algarve, Portugal, 1972

Marrakech, Morocco, 1970

Masai Woman in the Suburbs of Nairobi, Kenya, 1975

Arid Lake, Laguna Chapala, *Baja California, Mexico, 1972*

New York, 1970

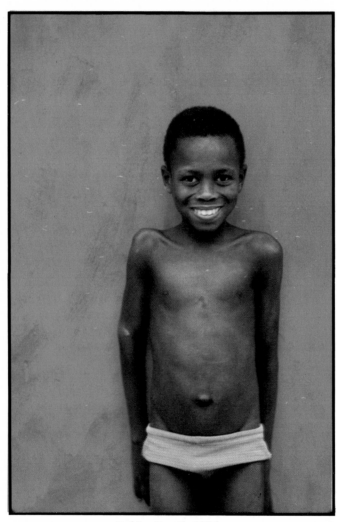

Bahia, Brazil, 1976

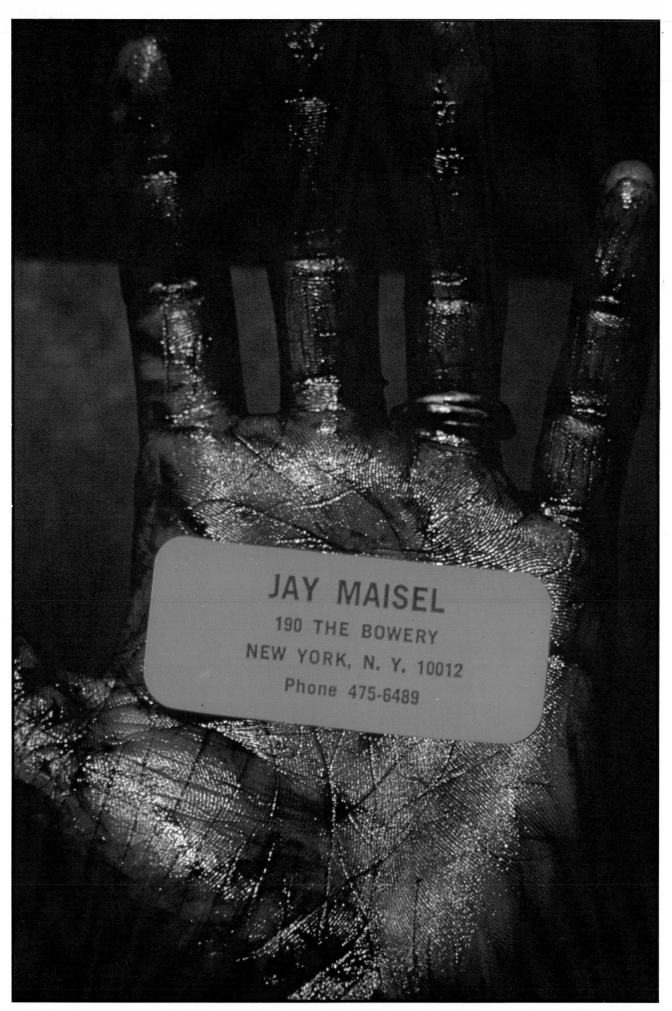

Aperture Transparency for a Show Window, New York, 1967

View from my Window, New York, 1977

London, 1965

tude." Paul Strand, another great "straight" photographer, said "I think that what exists outside the artist is much more important than his imagination. The world outside is inexhaustible. What a person feels about it is not inexhaustible at all.". Maisel, similarly, ". . . would rather be affected by life than control it. I would rather have things happen to me than build images. You have heard some people say that they don't just take pictures, they make them. Well, I take them. When I photograph a subject, I would like the subject to dictate what the photograph looks like, not me. I don't want to be the most important thing in the picture."

A photographer's freshness and openness to what the world has to offer depend on what Maisel calls "being there," a concept he illustrates with a story about the red-and-blue New York skyline reproduced in this book. The unusual atmospheric conditions that made this incredible picture possible were the subject of serious New York photographers' conversations for weeks after it happened. "If you are out here shooting, things will happen for you," Maisel says. "If you're not out there, you'll only hear about it."

He follows his own advice and is seldom without one or more cameras. When he is not on assignment out of town, he is usually on the streets of New York (or above them in a helicopter) shooting pictures for himself. When he is, literally, "at home," at the Bank, he is sequestered in his sixth-floor lair—the editing room. Easily the most important room in the building, the editing room is combination office, four-walled bulletin board, entertainment center, command post and refuge from thousands of everyday business details that would distract him from the other vital part of his work, the post-facto selection of im-ages—the editing process. A sign on the door reads "Editing Is Next to Godliness' and Maisel clearly believes it. Editing pulls together all the elements of the photographer's vision and focuses them directly on the latest batch of processed transparencies. For Maisel, it's the ultimate third degree for the photograph; it must pass muster on myriad of standards, time and time again. A single slide may be projected seven, ten, twenty times, before it is accepted or rejected by Jay's discriminating eye.

Although he rejects the idea of "correct" exposure or "right" color, he assumes responsibility for every square inch of his image. "Everything in that frame works for you or against you. Nothing is neutral. It is your responsibility because the camera is basically dumb—dumb like a hammer, which doesn't care if it hits the nail or your thumb. The camera can't differentiate between figure and ground; the photographer has to point it and do what he has to to make a meaningful image."

For Maisel, a meaningful image may be informational—about the sub-ject depicted, or it can be photographic—using the subject as a starting point for a picture that makes a visual statement about the medium of photography. The most successful pictures, obviously, are those that combine the two, but Maisel adds yet another element that he considers essential to a great photograph. He calls it "incident," "moment," or "climax," a particular presence in the photograph which either defeats our expectations or fulfills them so completely that the effect is arresting. The "moment" for Maisel is often an unexpected juxtaposition of color, an eloquent human gesture, or a small formal note that, once recognized, charges the composition with vitality, rendering the dozens of other frames Maisel may have of the same subject flat by comparison. Often, the climax of a Maisel picture is the light itself, and the ways light transforms and creates nuance in colors.

He defends his devotion to "color as content" against detractors who insist that color is a seductive peril to serious artistic expression, that a color photograph should stand on formal grounds even if the color were somehow drained out of it. Maisel counters without hesitation: "I make no apology for the pure joy of color for its own sake. I speak out for the joy of yellows, the passion of reds, the moods of blues." And, somewhat more prosaically, "I love color and am aware of the seductive dangers it poses to photographers, but I feel what's wrong with a little seduction?"

The benefits to be gained from the beautiful distractions of the world is at the heart of any message in Jay Maisel's photographs. Despite the chaos we know exists in the world, we should be able to recognize and appreciate—even revel in—the thousands of beautiful moments that occur every day. Many photographers disagree with this perspective. In the early '60's Maisel carried on a series of "wars," verbal polemics about the nature and responsibility of photography, with respected photographer Gary Winogrand. Although their attitudes were diametrically opposed, each held the other's work in high regard, and though they had little contact over the years, the two remained "arguing friends." Describing his younger colleague as ". . . a good photographer born at the wrong time, [who] would have been better off in the Renaissance period," Winogrand compared their photographic and world outlooks with these words: "Jay wants a perfect picture and I don't. I think perfection is death. He wants all things to be perfectly organized. This has nothing to do with life. We're living in a circus. Jay doesn't realize this."

But Maisel's photographs indicate that he does see the world as a circus; he simply responds to it differently. Like a child, he is thrilled and fascinated by what he sees, and with childlike generosity, he wants to share that vision with others. Sharing visual sensation is one of Maisel's espoused motivations for taking photographs. Claiming a poor visual memory, he feels a need to validate current visual experiences with a tangible record, to be reviewed later by himself and others. His acquisitive nature compels him to collect images "for loving inspection later on." His compulsion for his work has rewarded him richly both emotionally and financially.

Financial success in photography is virtually synonymous with the name Jay Maisel, though other top pros command equal or higher fees. His reputation rests largely on the fact that he is a tough negotiator with a sharp eye on the bottom line, although he denies having exceptional business acumen. "People always say I'm so good at business, but it's just that most photographers are so bad." In less modest moments, he admits his fondness for the give and take of the business of photography, and attributes his success to a willingness to walk away from a deal he considers unfair. His philosophy is pure and simple: "If you are afraid to lose, you can't make a good deal. If you're not afraid to lose, you can't make a bad one." His reputation as a fierce defender of photographers' rights, especially in the area of copyright, has earned him deep respect among fellow photographers.

Maisel parts company with many of his contemporaries, however, in his attitude toward his commercial work. Although he nurtures the ideal of pursuing his personal photography exclusively, his pragmatism (and his enormous overhead) obliges him to fulfill assignments on a regular basis. Unlike some others, however, he approaches his commercial work with the same passion that infuses his personal shooting. In fact, he believes that assignment photography, in many cases, enhances his photographic vision by enriching his overall level of experience. His eyes literally sparkle when he describes the incredible scenes he's had the opportunity to see first hand—the fiery "hell" of an old-fashioned steel mill, the quarter-million-dollar Calma computer screen that has a variable for over two hundred color combinations, or his all-time favorite, an off-shore oil rig. Being a professional photographer given access to places most people never see, he says, is "like having a license to steal experience."

Determined to bring more than just his camera equipment and film to a job, Maisel feels that satisfying the client is only part of his responsibility. If the photographer pleases himself as well as the client, then the work is truly a success. To that end, he often works twelve to fourteen hours a day, shooting an enormous amount of film, offering the widest variety of solutions to the situations at hand. The wise client, he believes, is one who capitalizes on the photographer's intellectual and artistic input, otherwise he is not getting his money's worth. His professional attitude and devotion to the job have placed him in high regard within the corporate and advertising art buying community.

In the area of fine arts he stands, along with other pioneers in color photography, at the threshold of full acceptance. In 1977, when no New York galleries were showing the work of color photographers, he co-founded, with Ernst Haas and Pete Turner, the Space Gallery, devoted exclusively to exhibiting works in color. Over the years, a growing respect for the artistic potential of color photography has increased the demand for Maisel's dye transfer prints, though print sales still account for a limited percentage of his income.

Like many photographers, Maisel is uncomfortable with the subject of "Art" with a capital "A." Friend and fellow photographer Duane Michaels has said that anyone who says he knows what art is, is lying Recently, Maisel concurred, and added, "I don't find myself capable of understanding the meaning of "Art" anymore. To understand "Art" in today's world, one has to be political. I'm not political enough to play the games."

If he has difficulty describing or discussing art, he is less reticent when defining and identifying with the label "artist." "Most artists have an arrogance that says, 'When you see this the way I show it to you, you're never going to see the world again in the same way you saw it before'; that's what Picasso did, that's what Matisse did. They changed the way we experience the world. After Vivaldi, it changes. After Brahms and Beethoven, it changes. It's never going to be the same again. The artist, whatever medium he's in, and whether he's aware of it or not, is insisting that this is the way you are going to see the world in the future. You may go back to your own way of seeing for a while, but you're changed."

Maisel embraces the arrogance of the artist. His images insist that we acknowledge his way of looking at the world. The beauty they reveal may have the power to change the way we see it in the future.

During one of Jay Maisel's recent lecture/slide shows before an audience of professional photographers, he admitted, with characteristic candor: "I'm always amazed when someone asks me a technical question. I've never considered myself accomplished technically."

Like Edward Weston, Walker Evans, and other "straight" photographers of the past, Maisel believes that the tools and techniques available to the photographer should serve his artistic vision, not become an end in themselves. He is not in love with his equipment, although he owns a lot of it, and (with the help of several meticulous assistants) maintains it all in top operating condition. Dependability is the quality Maisel insists upon in his equipment.

He uses Nikon cameras, the F-3 SLR bodies, and has acquired an almost complete Nikon lens system. His favorite lenses include the 600 mm f 4 ED-IF, the 300 mm f 2.8 ED-IF, an 80-200 mm f 4 zoom, the 135 mm f 2, 58 mm f 1.2, the 25–50 mm zoom, and a 15 mm f 3.5 wide-angle lens. He has a number of custom-made cameras and lenses that he uses in both his personal and commercial work. A German-made 90 mm f 2.8 Macro-Kilar lens with custom mounting for use with Nikon bodies is a longstanding favorite with Maisel. He has been using it extensively in recent months to photograph close-ups of ice crystals frozen on his windows. Another unusual piece of equipment in the collection is the "crazy camera." A custom-built 35 mm body, fitted with a 4 × 5 "leaf-shuttered" lens allows flat field, undistorted exposure of a section of Kodachrome film 108 mm long by 24 mm wide.

He uses Kodachrome 64 film exclusively and freely. He explains his legendary film consumption: "If it's worth taking a picture of, it's worth taking two, and if it's not worth taking two, it wasn't worth taking one. If something's really good, I have no hesitation about shooting a whole roll on it." In his commercial work, he "brackets" everything, shooting the same scene at a variety of exposures to allow for a multitude of variables in every situation: "I have an idea of what can go wrong. That's why I'm bracketing the thing. I also have an idea of what can go *right,* if I bracket. What I'm not sure of is where that thing kicks in. It's not an exact thing with light; light is not exact when you're out in the real world."

His prolific film use also relates to a broader Maisel philosophy—the failure-to-success ratio in the equation of professional and personal performance.

"When you go out and shoot, you can, if you're careful enough, come back from the job with a very few rolls and everything will be perfectly exposed and everything will be perfectly framed. And if you do that, you know you're not really earning your money, because you should be trying harder and you should be failing some. You have to have a lot of "overage" so that your failures aren't the only thing you came home with. You've got to have a lot of things that were magnificent failures in order to have magnificent successes."

BIOGRAPHY

1931
Born in Brooklyn, New York, January 19.

1948
Graduated From Abraham Lincoln High School, Brooklyn.

1952
Graduated Cooper Union Art School (Painting)

1953
Graduated from Yale University, Bachelor of Fine Arts

1954
Began career as freelance photographer

1955
First One Man Show, Photographers' Gallery, New York, New York.

1956
Photography course with Alexi Brodovitch.

1967
Taught color photography at School of Visual Arts, New York City.

1969–1974
Taught color photography at Cooper Union Art School

1977
Opened the Space Gallery, New York, with Pete Turner and Ernst Haas.

1977
Awarded Cooper Union Art School's St. Gaudens Medal.

1978
Awarded The American Society of Magazines Photographers' Outstanding Achievement in Photography award.

1979
Awarded the Syracuse School of Public Communications' Newhouse Citation.

Is currently living and working in New York.

BIBLIOGRAPHY

Magazines

"Blacks in New York," *DU,* (March, 1965), pp. 152-168
"35mm in Night Town," *POPULAR PHOTOGRAPHY,* (August, 1965), pp. 60-85
"Interview Jay Maisel," *PHOTO TECHNIQUES,* (May, 1966)
"People of Paris," *HOLIDAY,* (May, 1967), pp. 50-61
"Focus on Jay Maisel," *POPULAR PHOTOGRAPHY,* (March, 1969), pp. 76, 101-106
"Maisel", *CAMERA,* (November, 1969), pp. 6-17
"Recent Work by Jay Maisel," *JAPANESE DESIGN QUARTERLY/GRAPHIC DESIGN,* (September, 1970), pp. 2-10
"In Camera—Jay Maisel," *ADVERTISING TECHNIQUES,* (June/July/August, 1971), pp. 23-26
"Jay Maisel," *CA ANNUAL,* (September, 1975), pp. 19-37
"Le Soux Enfer de Jay Maisel," *PHOTO,* (June, 1976), pp. 86-95
"Les Avions de Jay Maisel," *PHOTO,* (August, 1976), pp. 34-45
"New York à Ma Fenêtre," *PHOTO,* (March, 1977), pp. 38-55
"Paris," *CAMERA 35,* (April, 1978), pp. 32-45
"Maisel le Magnifique," *PHOTO,* (November, 1979), pp. 50-67
"Q and A Jay Maisel Interview," *AMERICAN PHOTOGRAPHER,* (June, 1979), pp. 32-36
"Jay Maisel," *GRAPHIS 206,* (1979/1980), pp. 498-513
"Jay Maisel, Interview by Sergio Dorantes," *CAMERA, ENGLAND,* (August, 1981), pp. 28-41
"Manhattan—Images of the City," *NATIONAL GEOGRAPHIC,* (September, 1981), pp. 316-343
"World of Photography—Jay Maisel," *THE PHOTO,* (#86, 1982), pp. 2374-2379
"Looking for the Light," *American Photographer,* (September, 1982), pp. 46-65

Books

Contributor to:
Harlem on my Mind, New York, 1968. Color photographs pp. 217, 219, 226, 253, 281
The Greatest Jewish City in the World, New York, 1972
Photographers on Photography, New York, 1976. "Jay Maisel Interview," pp. 58-65
I Grandi Fotografi Jay Maisel, Milan, 1982
America, America, 1983 engagement calendar
Celebration at Persepolis, New York
Great Cities Series, Time Life International
    Jerusalem
    San Francisco
    New York
    London
Wilderness Series, Time Life Books, Alexandria
    Baja California
    Snake River

© 1982 Gruppo Editoriale Fabbri S.p.A. Milan

Prentice-Hall, Inc., Englewood Cliffs, New Jersey 07632

This book is available at a special discount when ordered in bulk quantities. Contact Prentice-Hall, Inc., General Publishing Division, Special Sales, Englewood Cliffs, N.J. 07632.

Library of Congress Cataloging in Publication Data
Gruppo Editoriale Fabbri.
  Jay Maisel.
    "A Spectrum Book." (Great photographers series.)
    Bibliography: p.
    1. Photographers.   2. Photography.
3. Maisel, J.   I. Title.
0-13-509068-7

10 9 8 7 6 5 4 3 2 1

P
ISBN 0-13-509068-7

Prentice-Hall International, Inc., *London*
Prentice-Hall of Australia Pty. Limited, *Sydney*
Prentice-Hall Canada Inc., *Toronto*
Prentice-Hall of India Private Limited, *New Delhi*
Prentice-Hall of Japan, Inc., *Tokyo*
Prentice-Hall of Southeast Asia Pte. Ltd., *Singapore*
Whitehall Books Limited, *Wellington, New Zealand*
Editora Prentice-Hall do Brasil Ltda., *Rio de Janeiro*

Printed in Italy